CONTEMPLATIVE
MEDITATION

by
Fr Matthew ODC

*All booklets are published thanks to the
generous support of the members of the
Catholic Truth Society*

CATHOLIC TRUTH SOCIETY
PUBLISHERS TO THE HOLY SEE

CONTENTS

INTRODUCTION TO MEDITATION

Relaxation

I would like to say something to help people to get started on contemplative meditation. The first thing to bear in mind is the importance of being relaxed. Any kind of tension, of body and still more of mind, interferes with the smooth development of contemplative meditation and it makes us more or less unreceptive to the inflowing of God's light and love. In order to develop this relaxation we should remember it not only when we come to do meditation but throughout the rest of our daily life as well. We should keep in mind the importance of being relaxed in our daily work and make use of any spare moments when we have nothing in particular to do to get used to the idea of simply doing nothing.

Many people find it hard to do nothing. If they have five minutes when there is nothing in particular to be done they feel they have to start doing something. If they sit down on a chair they want to pick up a magazine, they want to switch on the radio or the television. They want to do something. The idea of just doing nothing seems foreign to them, and yet it is important not only to give our bodies rest but our minds also. It is important to be able to sit down now and again even if for only a few minutes and relax our bodies, let all our muscles go loose and limp, and also relax our minds, allow the mind to slow down. We are accustomed to a racing mind, one thing after another filling our minds, doing this, doing that, getting here, getting there. Our mind is running quite fast most of the time and we need to let it slow down. This we do by not deliberately following up any line of thought.

When you sit down quietly and feel you want to start thinking about something do not follow up the line of thought. By all means let thoughts come but let them go again. Let thoughts come to your mind, let them wander in and wander out but do not lay hold of them. Let your mind gradually subside. This is something one ought to do particularly on going to bed at night. That is the very worst time to start following up any line of thought. It will keep you awake. Let your mind go free-wheel. If thoughts come don't lay hold of them, don't start working on them, let them drift out again and in that way you will gradually get into the habit of letting your mind slow down. This relaxed attitude of mind will not make you inefficient at work. On the contrary, because it releases tension it will make you more efficient at work because your activities will flow very smoothly. If you remember this idea of letting your mind slow down whenever it does not have to work actively, you will be better prepared to enter into meditation.

In the beginning of meditation you sit in a comfortable position, whether it be in an armchair or perhaps best of all, on a meditation stool which is both comfortable and keeps the body erect and the mind alert. You relax your body. You convey the idea of relaxation and looseness and limpness to every part of your body. Feel yourself loosening out, and then let your mind go loose. Take your mind away from any definite thought. Don't follow up any thought. Let your mind go free-wheel. Thoughts will come and go, in fact you may find that your mind is infested by thoughts. It doesn't matter, let them be, take no notice of them.

To begin your meditation from that state you gradually allow your mind to quieten. There are various ways in which you can do this. A way some people find helpful is by noticing their breathing. I do not mean that you should breathe in any particular way, or do breathing exercises, but simply to notice your breathing, to be aware of it, to listen to it as your breath goes in and out. Get into the rhythm of your breathing and, as it were, let your mind go along with your breathing, in and out, and this tends to quieten your mind.

Use of Mantra

Most frequently, however, what people find helpful in quietening the mind is the use of a mantra. The word 'mantra' is a Sanskrit word and it indicates a word or a phrase or a simple thought not expressed in any detailed words, or a mental picture not examined in any detail. If it is a word or a phrase you gently repeat it in your mind but do not think about its meaning. It is important not to think about its meaning. You just hold it in your mind in order to quieten the imagination. It is something given to the imagination to quieten it. It has a kind of hypnotic or quietening effect on the imagination, but in this state a person is not in any sense under hypnosis. Let me first of all explain in much more detail about the use of this mantra.

Your mantra might be a phrase from The Gospels: 'Come to Me all you who labour' or 'I am the bread of life'. 'I will give you a living water'. 'Come Lord Jesus'. 'Heal my soul for I have sinned against You'. 'Into your hands I commend my spirit'. 'Lord Jesus Christ have mercy on me, a sinner'. Any phrase like that. Any invocation. You gently repeat it, or perhaps not repeat it but let it simmer on your mind. Let it rest on your mind, and all the time the intention or the leaning of your heart is out beyond it. You are not focusing your mind on the phrase, the focus of your mind goes out beyond the phrase, it goes out to God, but you are not picturing God, you are not having any kind of image of God, you are not having any definite thought of God.

As far as your thinking mind is concerned God means for you simply nothingness because He is the infinite, He is the unbounded, and so you reach out in your heart, in your will, beyond every distinct thought and every distinct mental picture and hold yourself in an attitude of attentiveness to the unbounded indescribable God. Now where is the mantra? The mantra is at one side. You are not particularly noticing it but you are aware that it is there and it is helping to keep your imagination steady. As the bent of your soul reaches out to God more securely, more firmly, you feel less need of the mantra which is like a kind of crutch to help you remain in this state of attentiveness, and as this state gets stronger the mantra gets lighter and lighter, it becomes vague. If it began by being a few words it tends to shrink into a single word, and even that single word begins to get vague and almost fades away. For example, 'I am the bread of life' might become just 'life' or 'bread', and then the mantra seems to recede into the background. In a vague way you know it is there but it seems far away because the bent of your soul is leaning towards God in a way that is not expressed by any thought or image.

Sometimes in fact the mantra might fade away completely and then you are in a state of pure consciousness, a state of what is called transcendence because you have transcended or gone beyond every thought and every image. That state might not last very long and you may find that you need to come back to the mantra again and rest on it awhile. When you thus come back to the mantra, come back only to the extent that is necessary to support your attention, do not go right back to the beginning when you had to use the mantra in a very distinct and obvious way. If it is sufficient to go back to the vague memory of the mantra, that will be enough perhaps to hold your attention, and if it is enough then do not take it up anymore strongly because it will only draw you away again from your silent attentiveness. The mantra does not have to be a phrase. It is all the better if you only need a word, a single word, and here too people will choose whatever word they like. It is more a matter of the sound than of the meaning. It is a good thing that a mantra should have a meaning but you do not think about the meaning. It does impress your subconscious mind but you do not think about it. For example, the word 'Domine'. Domine is a good sounding word, it has good vibrations. It means 'Lord' as calling upon The Lord, but you don't think of that, and yet that gets into your subconscious mind, and as the bent of your soul opens out towards God in attentiveness that word begins to fade. It gets weaker and weaker and it might fade away completely, but after a while you may need to come back and lean on it a little in order to keep your imagination steady.

Wandering Thoughts

Now the problem is, of course, the wandering thoughts that come to the imagination, because even with the use of a mantra a person will often experience considerable difficulty in coping with wandering thoughts. If these wandering thoughts stop your meditation completely so that you start thinking about them and not about your meditation we call them distractions because they draw you away, which is the meaning of the word 'distraction'. They draw you away from your meditation so that you are thinking about something quite different. As soon as you realise this the only thing to do is to begin your meditation again.

Frequently these wandering thoughts are present in your mind but they do not draw you away from your meditation because the basic attentiveness is still there even though you are aware of the many thoughts wandering round your mind, coming and going. They are something of a nuisance and you wish you did not have them and you may be tempted to try and get rid of them, which would be a mistake because you will not succeed in getting rid of them. The more you give them your attention in order to try to get rid of them the worse they get because you are focusing your attention on them and you are distracting yourself from your meditation.

So long as there is this basic attentiveness to meditation take no notice of the wandering thoughts, let them stay there, and go on with your meditation. By which I mean hold yourself in that attitude of attentiveness to God beyond all thoughts and images and you will find that the wandering thoughts will come and go, and eventually they will tend to fade away because you are not giving them any attention. The less attention you give them the more they will fade away. So keep your attention on the meditation itself.

Other Forms of Mantra

Not only can a person use a phrase or a word for a mantra, he can also use a simple thought, so simple that it is not expressed in words, or only in very vague words. The thought, for example, of the presence of God. Just that God is here. God is all around you. God is within you. You are immersed in God. You are enveloped in God. Without going into all these words that I have to use to explain the idea, you hold the feeling of being in God and God being in you. That acts as a mantra, but you don't start thinking about it. You don't start thinking what it means or how you should appreciate it or what you should do about it. You don't go in for any of these reflections. Just hold the very simple idea and then you reach out beyond it. The whole aim is to reach out beyond into the great unknown, into the great infinity.

Then too, particularly if a person has a very vivid imagination or a very active mind, it is sometimes good to choose a scene for a mantra, a picture say from the life of Christ. One that often comes to my mind is the picture of Christ speaking to the Samaritan woman at the Well of Jacob. You can see Him there sitting on the low stone wall surrounding the well and the woman speaking to Him. And in connection with that you can also have the phrase in your mind 'I will give you a living water'. That is only one scene, but there are many from the life of Christ that you can hold in your mind, but do not start thinking about them. Of course you could; it is an excellent thing to think about various incidents in the life of Christ and to have reflections upon them, but that is discursive meditation and we are now talking about contemplative meditation.

So you simply use the mental picture of a scene in the life of Christ as a mantra, holding it there to give your imagination something to grasp at, with the word 'I will give you a living water', and while that picture and those words are in your mind your heart is reaching out beyond, into the infinity of God, and according as your heart reaches out, according as this attentiveness gets stronger and stronger and more stable the picture fades away and even the words fade away, or perhaps they just remain in a very vague way at the back of your mind... living water... living water, just resting your imagination gently on those words but reaching out beyond them. Sometimes, then, the words will fade away completely and you are in a state of entire transcendence. Sometimes you have to come back to your mantra, come back to the scene or the words, but in the gentlest possible way, just in so far as is necessary, and you then await the opportunity when you can go away again into that great unknown. That is the use of the mantra.

THE ESSENCE OF MEDITATION

The purpose of the mantra is to quieten your imagination so that the attentiveness of your heart can develop - that is where the real meditation lies. It is the focusing of our will on God. I use the words 'heart' and 'will' with the same meaning. They are really the same thing. It is the deepest thing within us, our will. The deepest leaning of our being, the reaching out of our inner being towards God. You can call it the will or you can call it the heart. You can think of it as the weight of our being. It is as though we were throwing our weight upon God. Imagine a person throwing the weight of his body up against a door; and we are throwing the weight of our being against God, just letting ourselves fall upon God. That is what I mean by focusing our heart or our will upon God. That is the essence of meditation because it means that we are desiring God, we are wanting God, we are open to God, we are listening to God, we are waiting upon God, we are surrendered to God. The word 'surrender' expresses it well; the surrendering of ourselves, the throwing of ourselves into the arms of God.

Loving Attentiveness

Now all these words I use in order to try to convey the idea of loving attentiveness. That is the expression that St John of the Cross uses, a loving attentiveness. It is an act of our will, an act of our heart. And when I say attentiveness to God I do not mean God in any way we can picture or imagine Him. As far as our imagination goes or our thinking goes it is nothing. We are being attentive to nothing, to no thing, to nothing we can picture or describe because we are going beyond all that. We are being attentive to a Being that is beyond all thinking and beyond all picturing and therefore we do not try to think or picture, and whatever thoughts or pictures come into our mind we take absolutely no notice of them, we just reach out in love; peaceful, quiet and attentive. That is contemplative meditation.

How God Comes to us

We do not expect anything to happen. When we are in that state we are not expecting to receive any extraordinary communication from God or any extraordinary enlightenment or feelings. We are not expecting anything to happen for the simple reason that everything is happening. God is working deep in our soul. While we are in that quiet attentive state God is doing His work. We need not wait for anything to happen because it is happening. He is doing His work in the unconscious part of our soul, deep down in the spirit, so deep that our conscious mind is not able to grasp what is going on. If our conscious mind were able to grasp what was going on it would be superficial, but because it is so deep it is beyond our perception.

So we are content to wait, in faith, completely happy that God is doing His work, His work of sanctification, His work of cleansing our soul from our failings and imperfections, of sanctifying us and increasing His divine life within us. That work that He Himself knows, that work that He has planned, He is doing it within us because, now, we have left ourselves completely at His disposal, not getting in the way with unnecessary activity of mind, with useless thinking. We are not getting in the way. We are leaving Him completely free to do His work.

Sometimes, frequently enough, He does give us feelings, especially a feeling of peace, a wonderful feeling of calmness, an awareness that He has a grip on us, that He is holding our attention, and deep in our heart we know that something very wonderful is taking place. And sometimes He will give us feelings of love, feelings of praise. In fact, from that deep contact that takes place between God and ourselves He sometimes inspires us to praise Him, to express our love for Him in words, or to express our sorrow for sin, but it is not we who are doing it then, and it requires no forcing or deliberate effort on our part, it is something that wells up spontaneously from the depths of our soul. We don't decide whether we are going to do it or not. All we aim at doing is being completely in the hands of God and if God wants us to use our mind in an active way, He does so.

We are like musical instruments and God is the Musician. We are at God's disposal and God plays upon us whatever melody He wishes. He can leave us in complete quietness and utter peace without anything tangible whatever, or on the other hand He can inspire us to praise Him in many different ways. Whatever it is, it is God who does it. We have done our part in placing ourselves in His presence and leaving ourselves at His disposal, and that is all that is required of us in contemplative meditation.

Harmonising Our Daily Life with Meditation

In meditation we direct our attention towards God and we withdraw our attention from everything else. Although thoughts might come to our mind we keep our attention directed towards God. Whenever we are distracted by any kind of wandering thought we come back as soon as possible to our attentiveness to God. The essential effort of meditation is to keep our heart thus attentive towards God, not in a way that is expressed by thoughts or mental images but simply an attentiveness to that great unbounded infinity that is beyond all thought and all image, an attentiveness to God not circumscribed in any way. And the more our attention is directed to God the more we are free from the binding and distracting influence of other thoughts and desires. So it is what *'The Cloud of Unknowing'* says, a reaching out to God in a cloud of unknowing and putting all other things behind us in a cloud of forgetfulness. That is our attitude in meditation.

Harmony of Life

But it is necessary also that that attitude be carried in a practical way into our daily life. It is not enough to aim at being attentive to God in time of meditation if we allow our desires to wander freely upon everything at other times outside meditation. There must be this harmony in our life as far as possible at all times. In fact, through the light and strength that we get in meditation we become enabled to develop a similar harmony throughout the rest of our lives, a harmony by which we keep our attention focused on God and withdraw our selfish desires from everything else. We must live a life that is directed towards God in which all the elements of our life are harmoniously ordered towards each other and towards God. It is through the grace that we get in meditation that we are enabled gradually to develop this harmony in our daily life, and as we develop it God comes through to us all the more strongly in time of meditation.

So it is not enough to be attentive at meditation; we must carry this same attentiveness over into our daily life. That does not mean that we have to be thinking of God always; we cannot, except by a very special grace, and even then it is not by discursive thoughts of the thinking mind but by a deep awareness of God's presence. But what we should aim at doing and what we should struggle towards achieving in ever greater perfection is harmony in our lives, which means that everything in our life should be directed towards God, and done in order to please God. We can see that clearly enough when it is a matter of avoiding anything that would be in any way sinful. We know very well that such a thing could not be offered to God.

But when it is a matter of things that are good in themselves we are often not so clear. Many people have the idea that self control is artificial; it implies a certain 'force', and they think they ought to be spontaneous, that life should be a spontaneous growth, a spontaneous development, and that anything that would hinder this spontaneity is in some way wrong.

Self-Discipline

To think that way is a failure to recognise the kind of nature we have. Our nature is not in its perfect state. It is in a disordered state as a result of Original Sin. Therefore we have the obligation of controlling what is disorderly so that our true nature may freely express itself. I think it was St Thomas who defined freedom as the joyous and spontaneous self-expression of a perfect nature. You can easily see what a wonderful definition that is. A perfect nature, joyously and spontaneously expressing itself, just pouring itself out, without any inhibitions, without any frustrations, without any limitations.

But note, he says 'a perfect nature'. Our natures are not perfect, they have been wounded by Original Sin, and if we allow ourselves to express what we feel and what we want to do, spontaneously, evil will come out as well as good. The disorders of our nature will make themselves felt and they will often suffocate what is good and orderly. So we have to exercise control, we have to exercise a discipline on the disorderly elements of our nature, that is to say, on anything that is self-centred, in order that our true nature may be allowed to develop and express itself towards God.

Getting Our Priorities Right

Spontaneity comes gradually according as our souls come under the influence of the Spirit of God. Then we are able to be spontaneous because it is the Spirit of God within us that becomes the motive power of our actions and of our thoughts, and not our own selfishness. We have to work towards this by ordinary discursive reflections, we have to do some practical thinking, and we have to talk to God in ordinary words asking Him for help and guidance in this right ordering of our lives.

Contemplative meditation does indeed give us the urge for it, it gives us a certain instinct for it, but we have to do our practical thinking as well. We have to be sensitive to anything in our lives that is not pleasing to God. And not just the actual things, but our attitude towards them and to what extent we are doing them for our own sake, or for God's sake. And here it is a matter of putting everything in its proper place. Our lives should be a harmonious whole and, as such, directed towards God.

In other words, we have to watch our priorities. What do we regard as the important things in our daily life, and are we giving them the place that they ought to have? Are we doing things which are good in themselves but which are crowding out other things that are more important? Are we doing certain good things just because we like doing them when we are neglecting other good things that we ought to be doing? Not that it is wrong to do things that we like doing. But even those things we like doing, we should do them not precisely because we like doing them but because God wants us to do them.

Many of the things God wants us to do are enjoyable, they are pleasant, and we derive great personal satisfaction from the doing of them, but we are not to do them precisely for the sake of the satisfaction that we get out of them, we are to do them for God. And doing them for God we have every right to enjoy the pleasure and the satisfaction that they give us, but without turning to grasp at the pleasure. There is a big difference between enjoying the work we do and grasping at the pleasure of it. When we enjoy the work we do for God it is God we should be thinking of, our joy should be a joy in serving God. We should praise Him, and thank Him that we are working for

Him, we should keep our attention directed towards Him since we are doing His work and are happy to be doing it. We praise Him for the happiness He gives us. Our attention is on Him, and we are not turning round to fix our attention on the pleasure we are getting, to grasp at it, to clutch it to our hearts, because if we do that we are turning away from God, and if we turn our attention away from God we are turning away from the source which gives us that pleasure and that satisfaction, and we find that, very quickly, it dries up.

Whenever we clutch at any happiness for its own sake it begins to dry up, because we are seeking something in it that we ought to be seeking only in God. But when we cling to God, then we find that the fulfilment of His will gives us abundant pleasure. So then, it is a matter of getting right order into our life.

SETTING ASIDE TIME FOR GOD

Some people think that if they want to fit in something like meditation into their life, and they are already living a very busy life, that they have to put it in addition to everything else. They think they are going to get up earlier in the morning, or they are going to go to bed later at night in order to fit it in, but they very soon realise that they cannot do that, that they need their sleep. They get over-tired, and it does not occur to them that if they are to fit in something for God such as regular meditation or spiritual reading, into a life which is already very well filled, they have to leave out something, and they have to make up their minds what it is they must leave out.

Sometimes a very good thing has to be left out. You might be helping people, doing a lot for people who are in need, but you have to decide what you are going to leave out if you are going to give time to God. It is a mistake to think that God does not mind as long as you are doing good to people. It is excellent to do good to people, but God has a right to claim some of your time for Himself. When Christ was in His public life He spent all day doing good for people, healing their diseases, casting out devils, and the crowd so pressed upon Him that He had scarcely time to eat, but yet He found time for prayer. He would go up into the mountains at night, and even spend whole nights in prayer to God. Now we are not likely to be able to spend whole nights in prayer, we need our sleep, but we must find time for it.

We must find time to give to God alone. Because if we don't keep ourselves in contact with the source of all goodness, with the source of our being, then we shall not have within us what we should give to others. We may succeed in giving them some kind of material assistance, material consolation, ordinary human comfort, but we shall not be channels of the grace of God for their souls if our own souls are not steeped in the grace of God. And so it is that we aim at directing our lives to God outside the time of meditation.

Spirit of Sacrifice

That will often require sacrifices to be made, and we shall come to see in our meditation that there are certain things God is asking us to do, or certain things He is asking us to change or give up, and they might be good things. It is easy to see that God would ask us to give up something that is wrong or sinful in some way, but when it is something good it is not so easy to convince ourselves that God wants us to give it up. And why would He want us to give it up? Simply because, although there is some good there to be done, we may not be the people He wants to do it. He may want somebody else to do that work. He may have some other plan for the particular individual that we are helping, but He wants us to do something different, and we must be sensitive to His guidance.

When God gives light to our soul in meditation, we must not turn away. How easy it is when a light comes to us, showing us something that we do not like, asking for something that we do not want to give, that we immediately find a reason for deciding that that is not genuine, God is not asking that. It is like the parable of The Sower, when he sowed some seed that fell by the wayside the birds of the air came immediately and picked it up, and it never grew. Similarly, when God inspires a person in their meditation to do something for Him, or give up something for Him, sometimes the Devil will put a thought into their mind telling them not to listen, that it is not God, He does not want that, that what they are doing is right and good. The Devil snaps the inspiration out of their mind and it never comes to anything. So, when God gives light in meditation, we must look at it. We must hold ourselves steady, and if we are doubtful we keep up our contact with God.

Being Open to the Light of God

We are not bound to take action about any inspiration until we are certain. When we are in a state of doubt we must hold ourselves steady under the inspiration, waiting for God to make it clear, waiting for God to give us the certainty that we need. And if we do hold ourselves steady, saying to ourselves, 'I am not sure whether I should do this, whether I should respond to this inspiration, whether it is really an inspiration or not or just my own imagination, but I want God to enlighten me. I will hold my attention under this light and I will ask God to make it clear, and as soon as He makes it clear, then, with His help, I will give Him what He wants'.

Let us hold ourselves steady under the light of God, which in the beginning, perhaps, might be so faint that we might be tempted to shut it out; but we do not shut it out, we do not turn away from it, we wait for it to grow and develop and get stronger, and eventually it comes to a point when we know, with absolute certainty, that God wants this, and we also know that we are going to give it to Him. Because, not only does this light increase in our soul, but the power, or the strength, that comes from Him also increases and we find that just about the time when we know with complete certainty that God is asking this we also find it in our heart to do it for Him. He has built us up. He has given us strength.

Sometimes there are things that in the beginning seem to be too much for us, we feel God could not be asking us to do them, but if we hold ourselves steady under His light we find not only that He is asking us to do them but that He has made us able to do them. And thus it is that, little by little, we get order into our lives, we get discipline into our lives. We think out how we ought to plan our day. Perhaps we work out some sort of timetable. A timetable really means that we think out beforehand what is the right way of spending our day, what are the right things to be doing at each particular time of day, always allowing for the fact that circumstances will arise to change situations. We cannot foresee everything, but we have a basic timetable by which we know that, barring unexpected intrusions, we ought to be doing certain things at certain times. When we arrange our time like that in advance, seeing things the way God wants us to see them, we can be assured that we are doing God's will.

Our Moods Give Way to God's Spirit

What carries us away from God's will is to leave
ourselves at the mercy of our whims and moods as
they arise. If a person has no fixed routine, no fixed
arrangements as to how to spend his day, he will be at
the mercy of any mood or feeling that comes to him,
he will do just what he feels like doing. Many people
think that that is a good thing to do, to do what they
feel like doing.

But that is giving way to selfishness, giving way to
moods, and that is not God's will. God has His plan for
us, and it is for us to submit ourselves to it, to submit
ourselves to God's arrangements, to submit ourselves
to the discipline of a life that is arranged according to
God's will. That will often go against our feelings, it
will often go against our moods, and yet gradually, our
own selfish moods and feelings will become
controlled. They will cease to trouble us as they did in
the beginning. Because we are not giving in to them
they get starved, they get worn out, they no longer
have the strength and the violence that they had
originally. In fact, they die away, and as they do so the
power of God's Spirit in us gets stronger, and the Spirit
of God becomes the inspiring power in our lives so we
find that we are free and spontaneous agents, that we

no longer have to 'force' because our spontaneity is coming from the power of God's Spirit within us and, to a very large extent, we are able to express that freedom which is described as the joyous and spontaneous self expression of a perfect nature.

True, as long as we are on earth our nature is not completely perfect, and we always have to be vigilant in self control. But because now our selfish desires are very much under control, and because the Spirit of God has got full power in us, we live with the spontaneity that comes from the Holy Spirit. It is the freedom of the Spirit by which we are lifted up above our own selfishness, and we enjoy all the wonder of a life that is spontaneous and joyous in the power of the Spirit of God. That is what we aim at. Contemplative meditation gets us going on it, keeps us going on it, gives us the light and gives us the power, but we do our own practical thinking in order to respond to that light, and bring the power of God's grace into every detail of our daily life.

DESIRE FOR GOD

Love is of two kinds, the love of desire and the love of goodwill. You can say that love is the response of our will to what is good, or the harmony of our will with Being, which means that we respond to the goodness of Being, to the attractiveness of Being. When we are attracted by a good that we do not as yet possess, we desire it. When we already possess the good the reaction of our will is to radiate it, to communicate it, to share it.

The Divine Attraction

When we enter into the silence of meditation the attractiveness of Being begins to exercise its influence on us. In fact, if we have the gift of faith there is a double attractiveness, the attractiveness of Being, namely God as manifesting Himself in the Universe, and the attractiveness of God in offering us a personal invitation to share His life.

Thus there is a double attraction and the last one is far stronger than the first. That is to say, the personal invitation that God has given us to share His own life develops a far stronger attraction than the other impersonal attraction where we are drawn to Him as the source of all being and the source of our own being. Corresponding with this magnetic pull from God there is what you might call a force of gravity at work within ourselves, a spiritual weight, that makes us want to fall into the centre of our being, that makes us want to fall into the source of our being, into God, and this double element, God attracting us and our desiring to fall into God, develops in us a strong desire for God, to possess Him and to be possessed by Him. It is when we are in the quietness of contemplative meditation that this attraction exerts its power.

We might wonder why this attraction is not always very evident, even in meditation, and the reason is that there are many other desires within us, desires for things that have no particular relation to God. If we desire something in order that it may lead us to God then of course it supports and helps our desire for God, but we desire many things that have no connection with God; these draw away our energies from God and we are, in fact, scattered over many different things. Even though we are not conscious of being influenced by various desires they are there within us, things that deep down unconsciously we are clinging to. We allow ourselves to be drawn away by the pleasures of life, by the cares of life, by the problems of life. These things get a grip on our minds, they absorb our attention a lot and so they draw away the strength of our desire for God. Therefore we need to get into the habit of turning our minds towards God and away from any other thoughts or desires that would distract us from Him. This is particularly the case at the actual time of meditation.

Distracting Thoughts

There are two kinds of distraction. In the first we are conscious of distracting thoughts but they do not really take us away from our meditation, and in that case we simply keep our attention on our meditation and ignore these thoughts. We don't even try to put them away because they are not injuring our meditation, they are just vaguely present but our attention is on our meditation. Then there are other distracting thoughts which really do distract us, which pull us right away from our meditation so that for the time being we are not meditating, we are thinking of other things. As soon as we are aware of such thoughts the only thing to do is to turn back again to our meditation.

But in order to keep our minds reasonably free from distractions we must at other times also try as best we can to turn our minds away from useless thoughts, not allowing our minds to get involved in any kind of thinking that is not serving a useful purpose. Useful thinking, certainly, that is part of God's will for us, but to be uselessly allowing our mind to dwell on things, or to dwell on them beyond the degree that is right and proper, is only drawing us away from God and lessening our desire for God. We shall never be able to eliminate all the wanderings of our imagination. God Himself will draw us away from them from time to time when He wishes.

Sometimes in the silence of meditation God absorbs our entire attention, He draws us into complete inner silence, but that is God's doing. It usually only lasts a short time, but for the most part our imagination wanders and no matter how much we may be detached from other thoughts we cannot really help this wandering of the imagination.

St Augustine describes the ecstasy he shared with his mother standing at a window in Ostia overlooking the harbour when they were about to sail from Italy back to Carthage. He describes how both of them together shared in the same ecstasy in which they gradually rose above all created things and eventually touched the supreme wisdom of God in an ecstasy of delight. But then he tells us what a let down it was to find themselves back amid the ordinary things of life. The ecstasy only lasted for a moment.

So normally we shall have to put up with the wanderings of our imagination even while we are being attentive, and deeply attentive, to God in interior prayer, but we can, little by little, by co-operating with God's grace eliminate those distractions that come from attachments, that come from the fact that we are preoccupied and concerned with our affairs. You might say that such preoccupation is necessary. Not really. We surrender these things to God and let ourselves be guided by God. God takes over. He guides us and we respond to Him, and we deal with our affairs far more efficiently like that than if we were to feel that it was up to us to look after them.

Where Happiness is Found

It is interesting to realise that we are not able to imagine perfect happiness. We have no experience of perfect happiness and we cannot conceive what it is like. Try any way you wish to imagine a state in which you would be perfectly happy and you will find disadvantages in it, you will find some kind of a snag somewhere; this is because perfect happiness is beyond our imagination. But it exists. It is God: Universal Being without limit. We never get to the end of it. We never reach a point where we can say "Is this all, is there no more?", there is always more. Complete fulfilment; it is in God we find it. That is why we ought to desire God above everything, and we ought to desire everything else only to the extent that it leads us to God. That means having harmony in our life with everything leading to a final purpose, an ultimate goal, something for which we are living and to which our whole life is leading. This something is God, and everything else is a step in that direction.

It is rather surprising when people sometimes say "Life is not worth living. What is there to live for?" Life is always worth living, there is always something to live for, there is God. God is the only reason why life is worth living. If there were no God life would not be worth living for anybody, but because there is God life is worth living for everybody regardless of what it is like because everything can be turned into a means of finding God. It does not depend on whether circumstances are favourable or not, on whether we seem to have opportunities or not. It does not depend on whether we have very favourable circumstances for

living a spiritual life, or whether the circumstances
seem to be all against us. That is not what is important,
what is important is how we react. It is by our reaction
to life, by our reaction to circumstances that we either
find God or lose him.

I think here of Richard Wurmbrandt who spent
fourteen years in communist prisons in Romania and
who suffered every kind of torture you can imagine,
indescribable torture - you would almost wonder how
the human mind could ever think of inventing them -
and yet it sanctified him. He reached tremendous
heights of holiness in his sufferings. Yet people will
say "Oh, but I can't find God if I am not comfortable. I
can't find God if I am suffering any aches and pains. I
can't find God if people are not reasonably nice to
me". We can find God always, everywhere, in everything,
as Richard Wurmbrandt certainly showed he could in a
very deep intense way.

"The prison years did not seem too long for me" he
says, "for I discovered, alone in my cell, that beyond
belief and love there is a delight in God: a deep and
extraordinary ecstasy of happiness that is like nothing
in this world".

So everything leads us to God if we react to it in the
right way, if we seek God in everything, if we try to

keep our feet on the path that leads to God. As St Paul says, "All things work together for the good of those who love God". So the desire for God and for making our way towards Him should be the consuming desire of our life. All our plans about our daily life, about our future, about what to do and what not to do, what job to have, where to go; all that should be inspired and guided by the question, 'Is it going to lead me to God?' 'Is it going to bring me closer to God?' 'Is it what God wants?' If we really desire what God wants God will see that we get it.

Informative Catholic Reading

We hope that you have enjoyed reading this booklet.

If you would like to find out more about CTS booklets - we'll send you our free information pack and catalogue.

Please send us your details:

Name ....

Address ....

....

....

Postcode...

Telephone...

Email ....

Send to: CTS, 40-46 Harleyford Road,
            Vauxhall, London
            SE11 5AY

Tel: 020 7640 0042
Fax: 020 7640 0046
Email: info@cts-online.org.uk